Nostalgic Christmas Coloring Book

by

Jen Moorelake

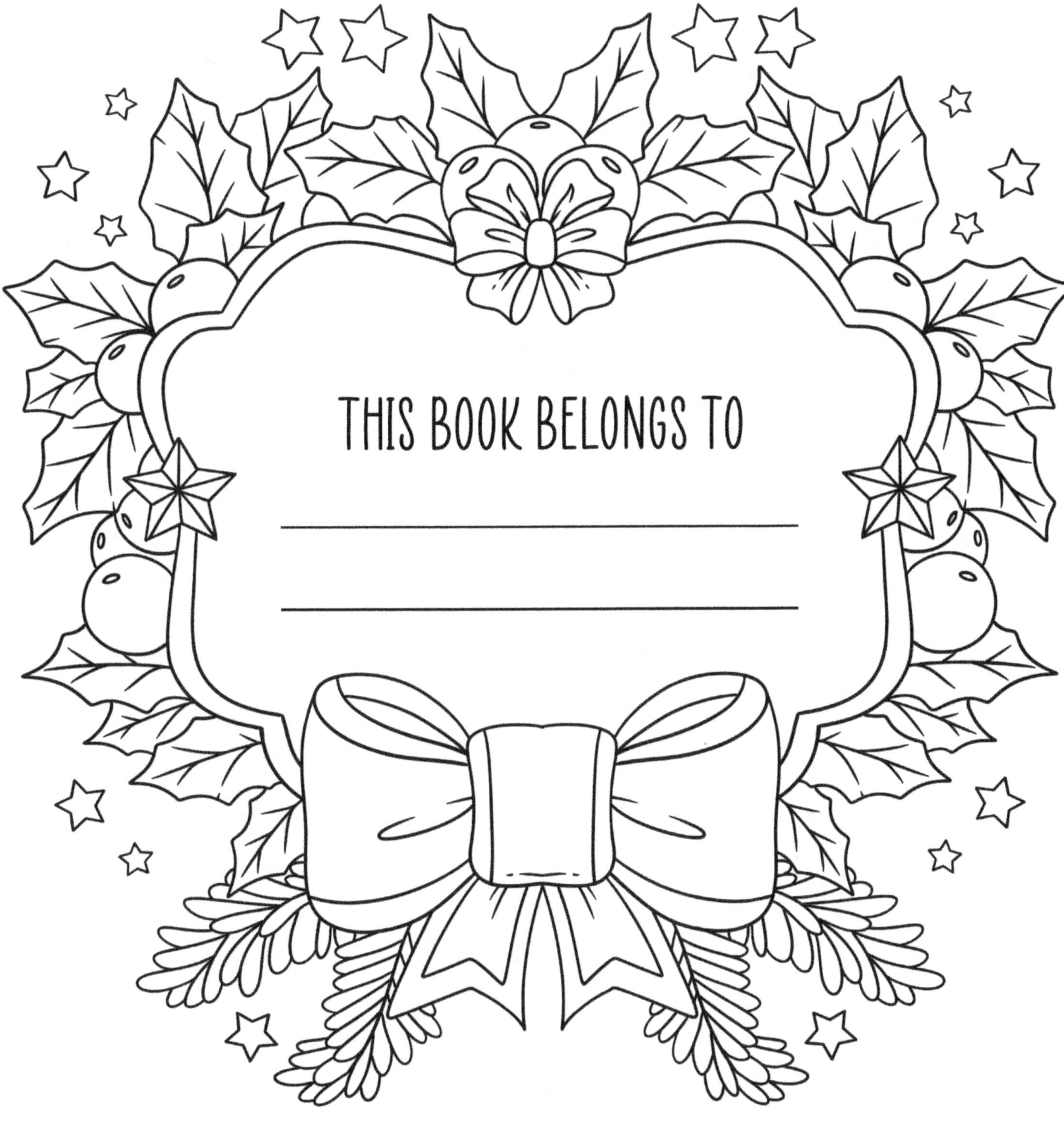
THIS BOOK BELONGS TO

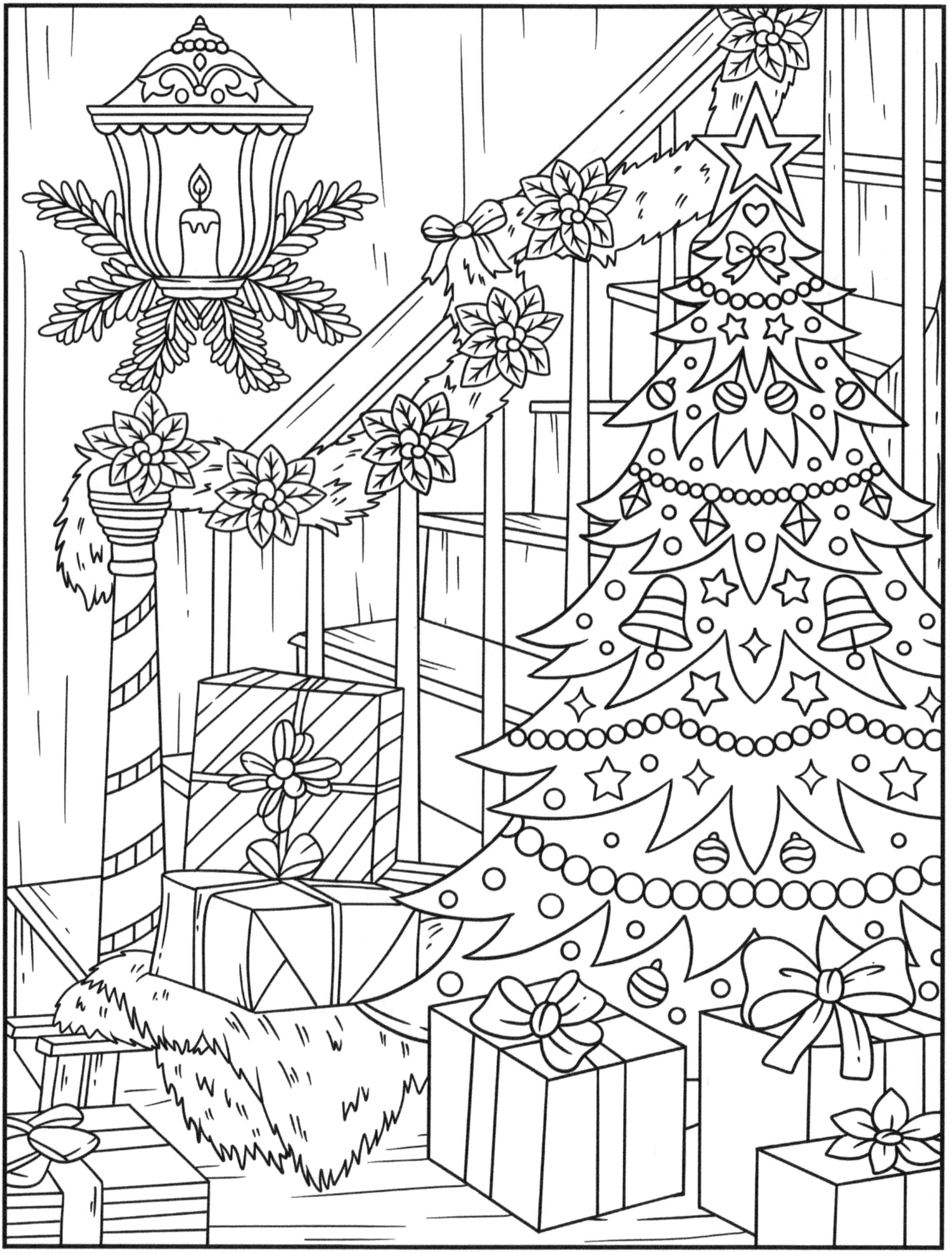

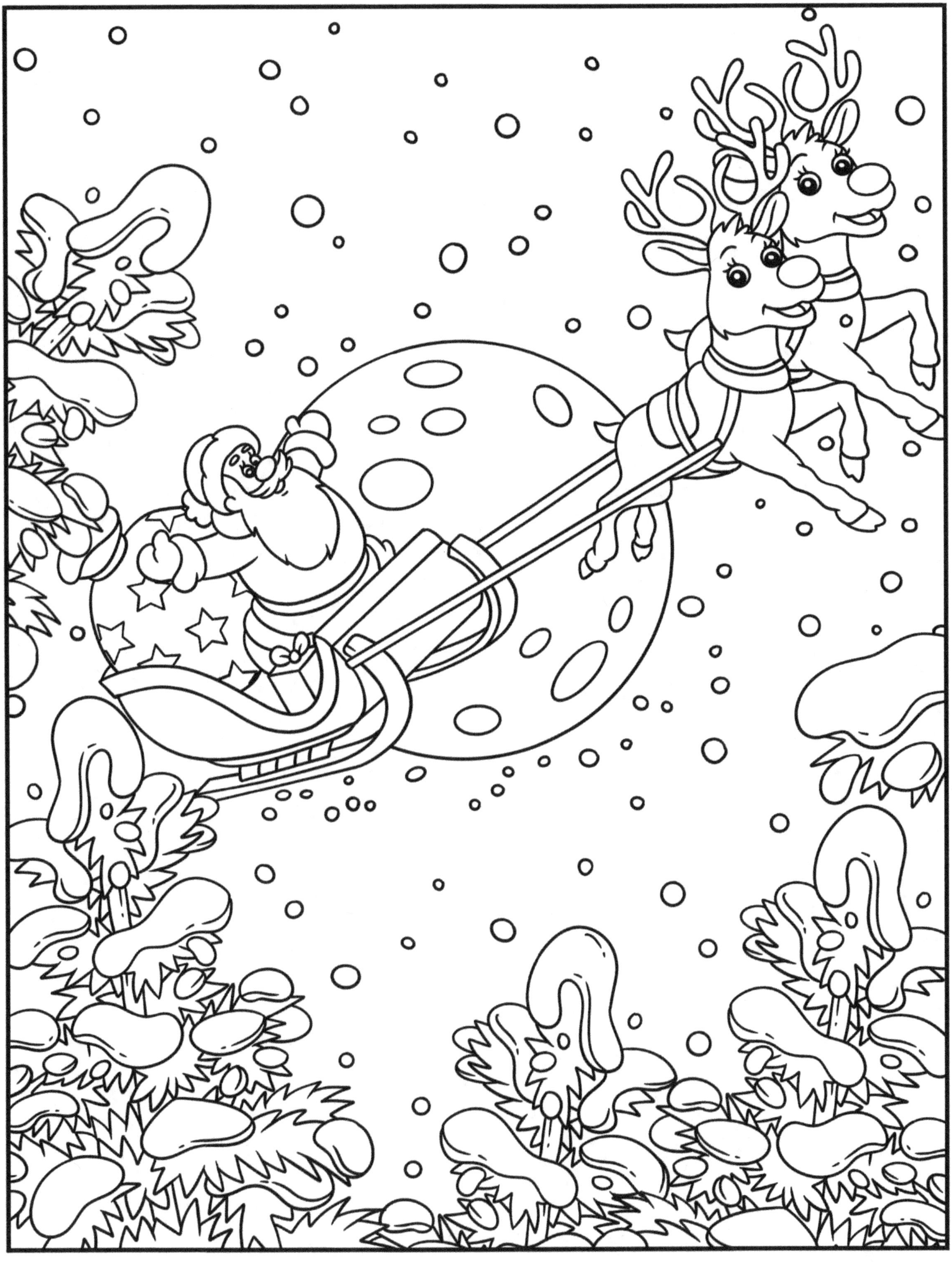

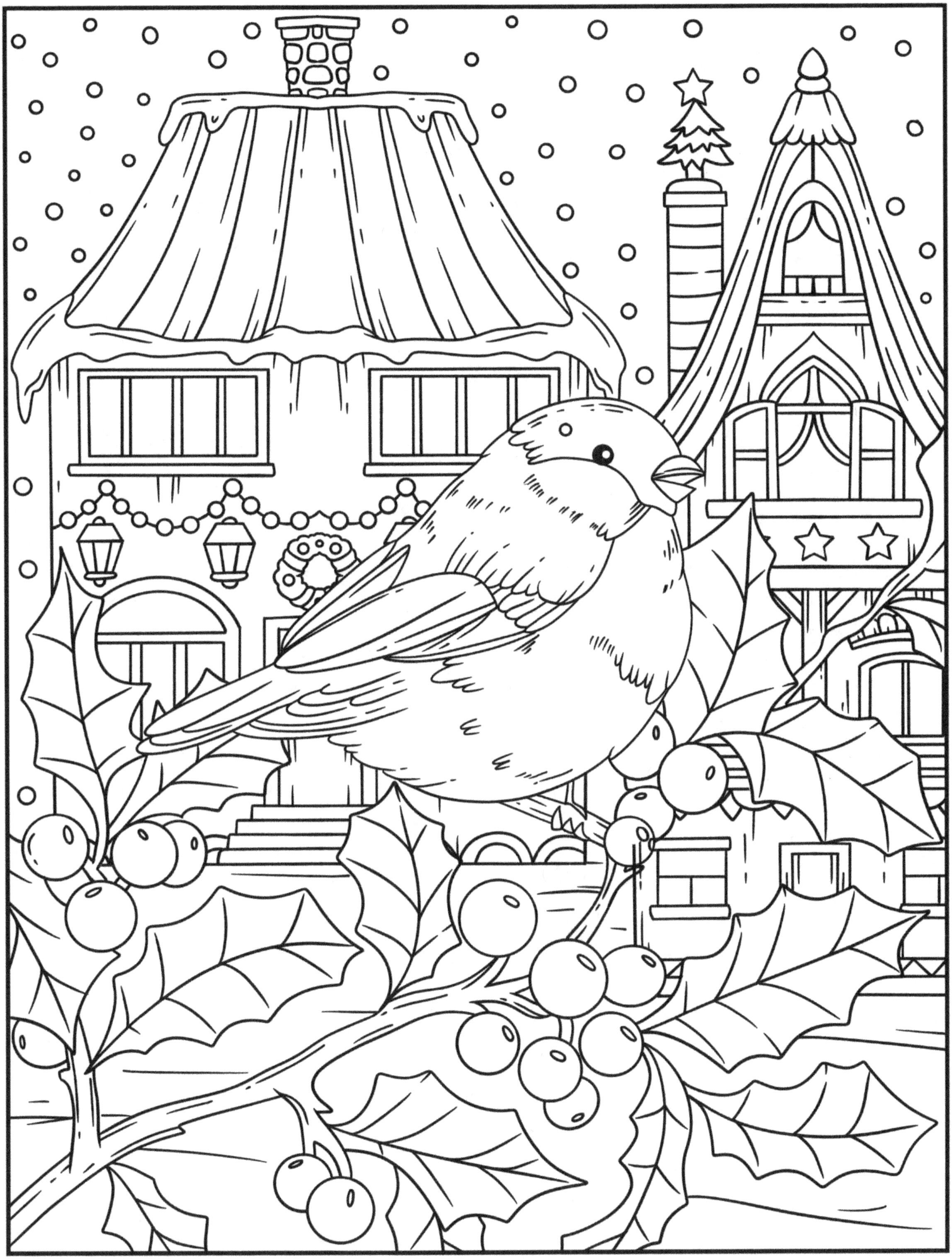

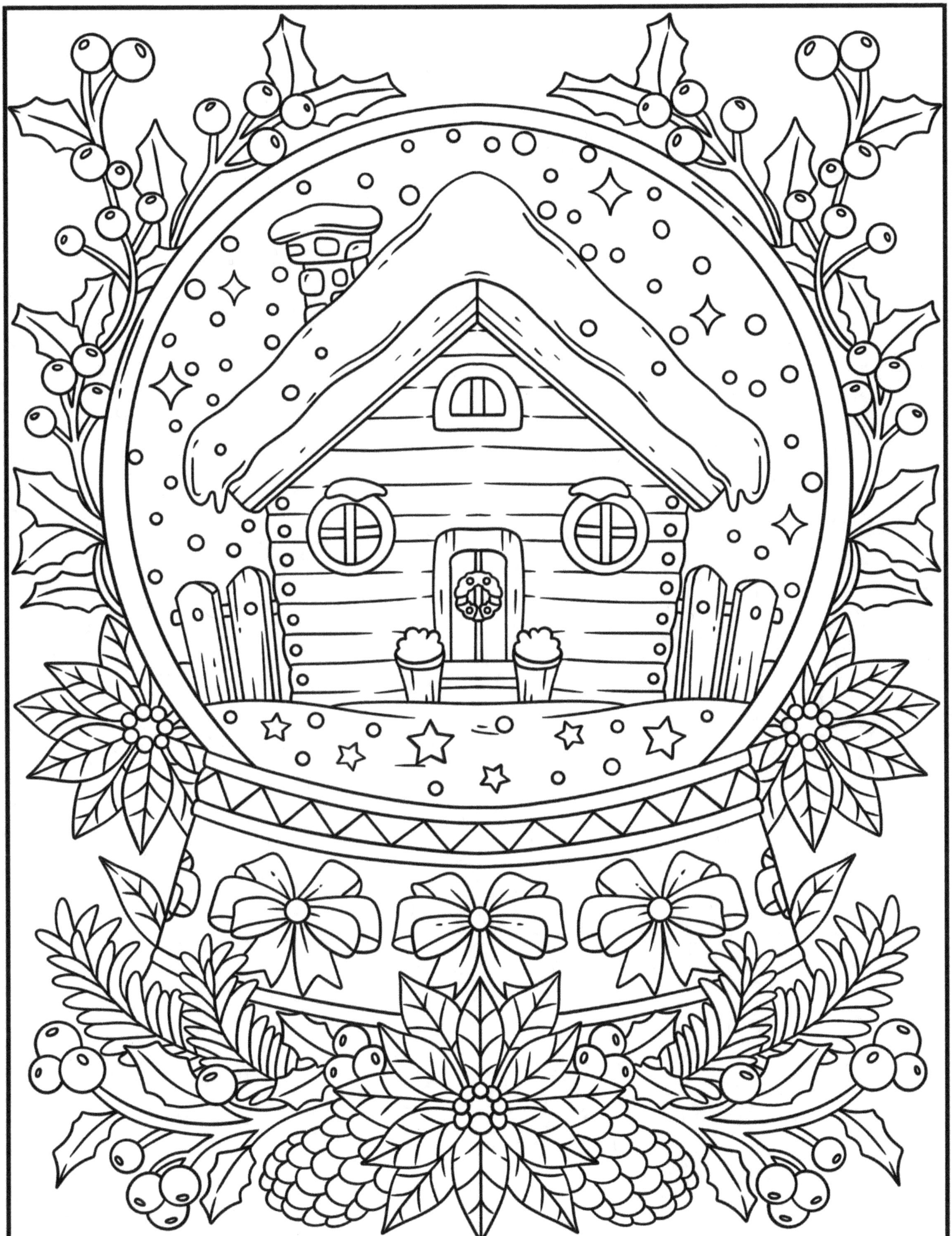

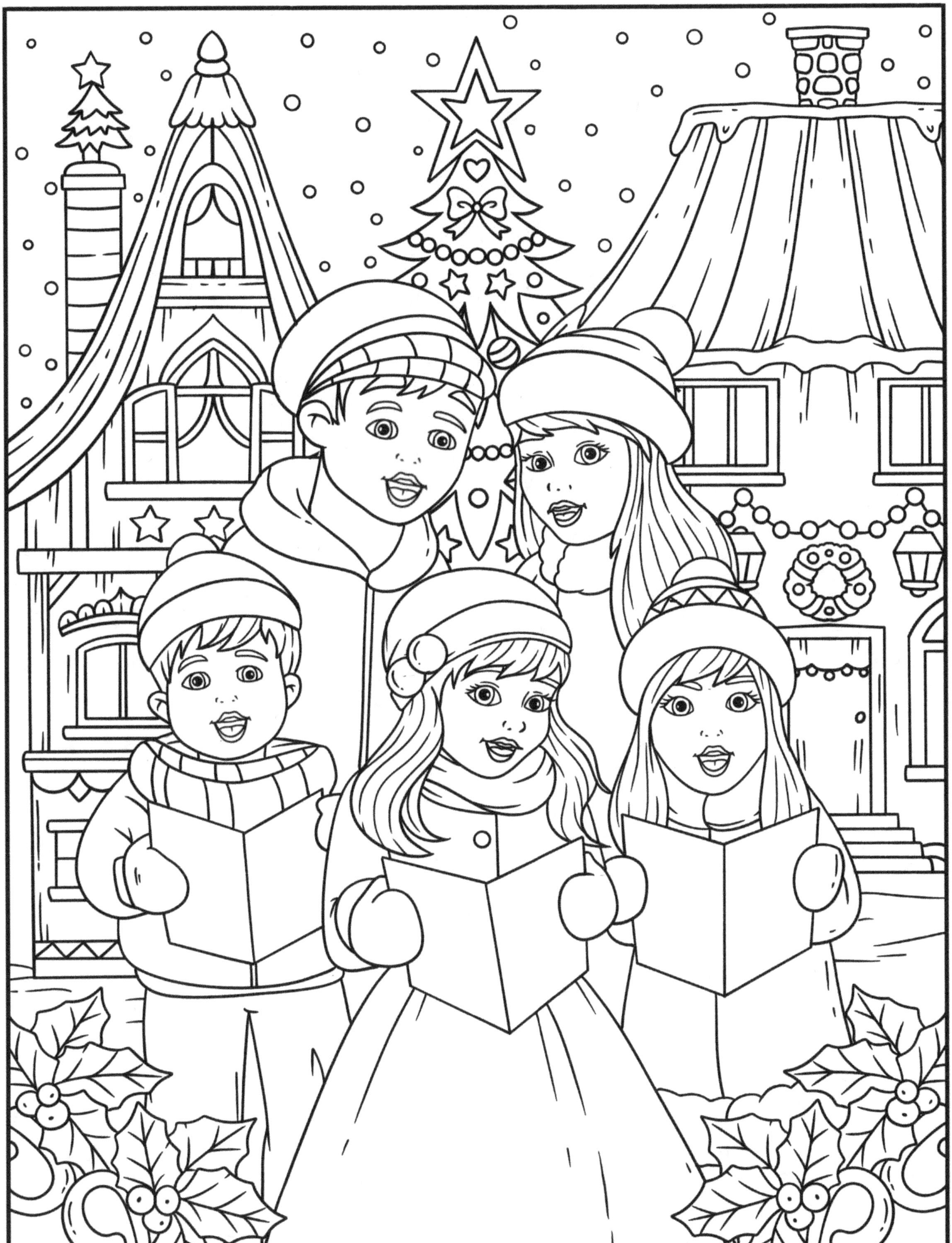

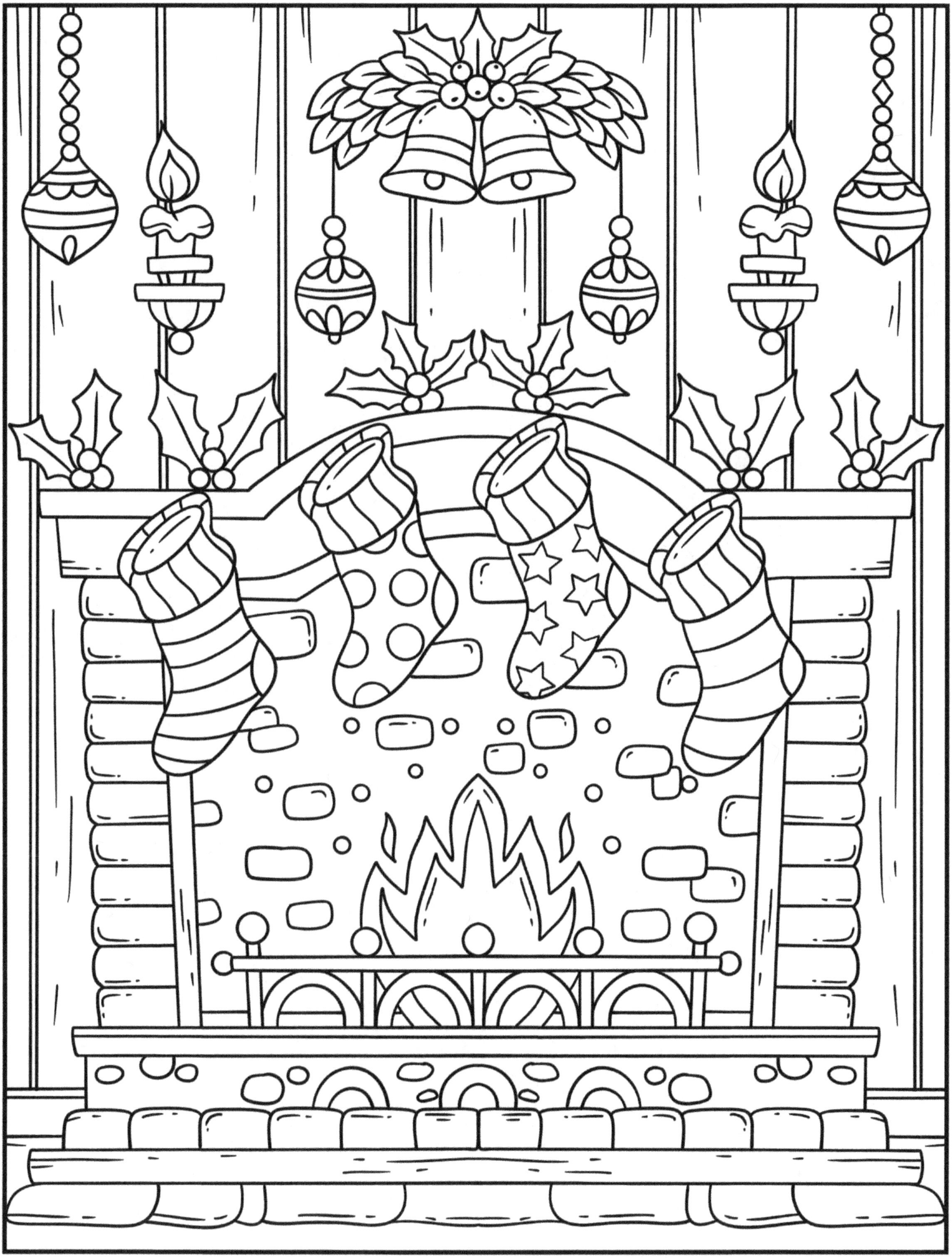

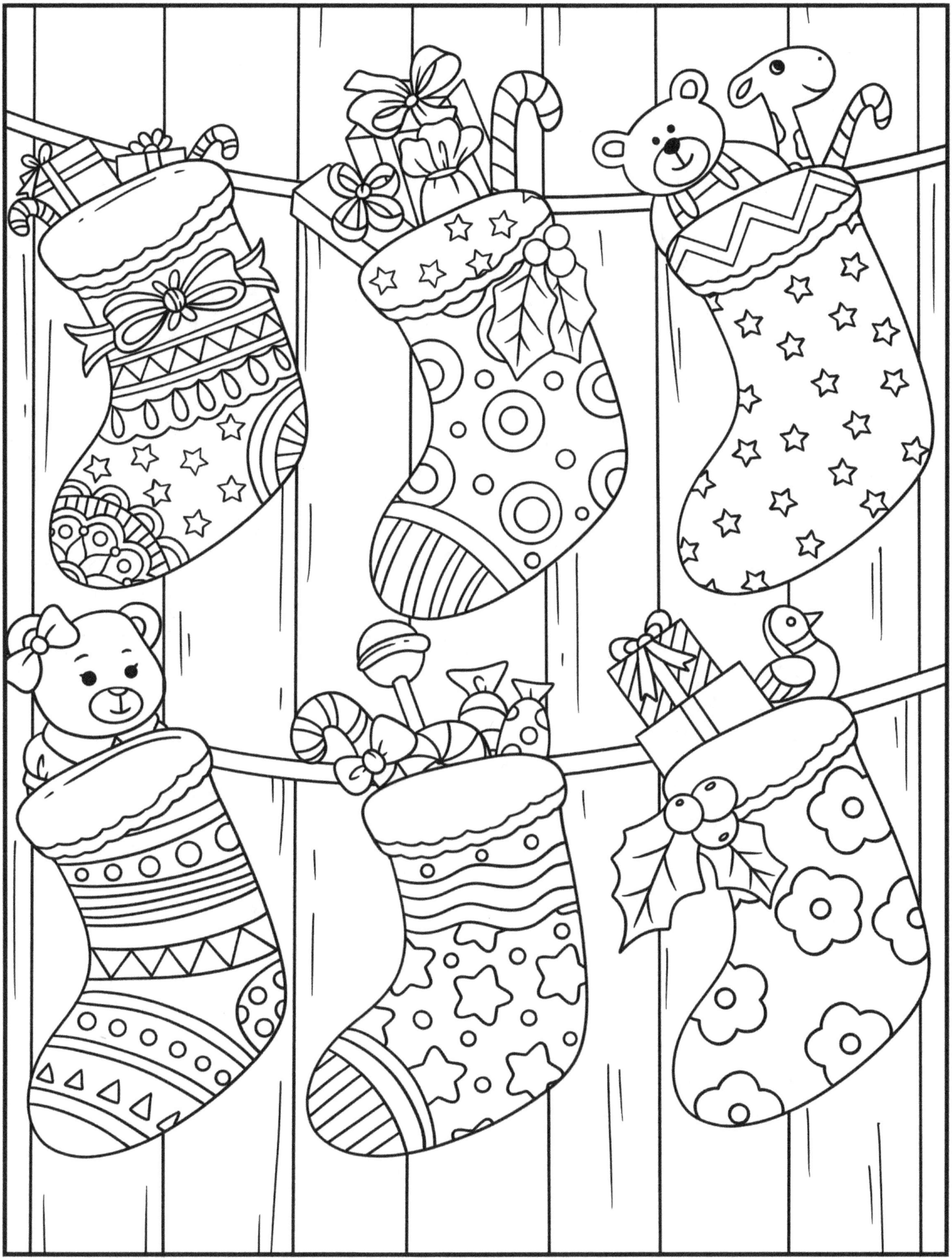

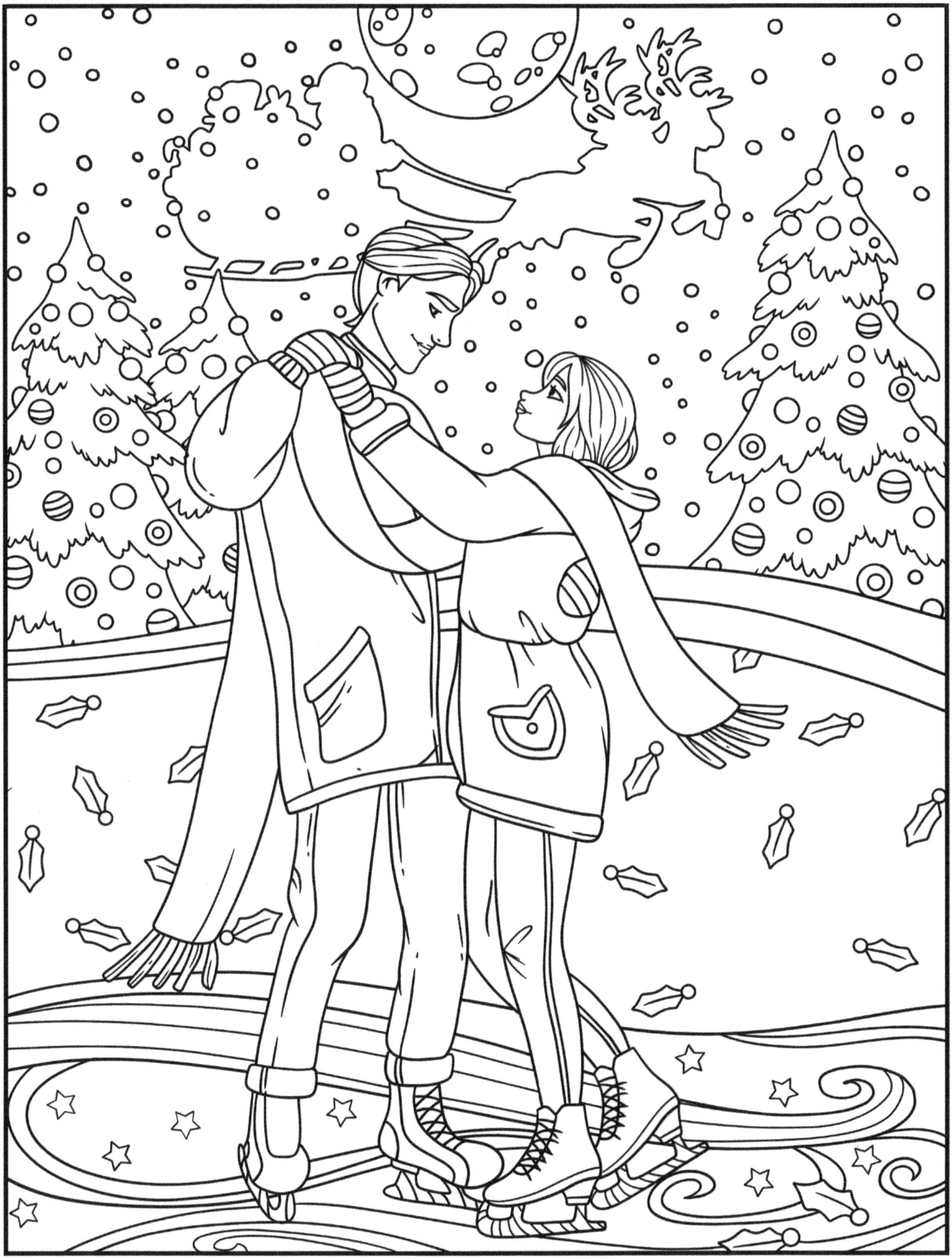

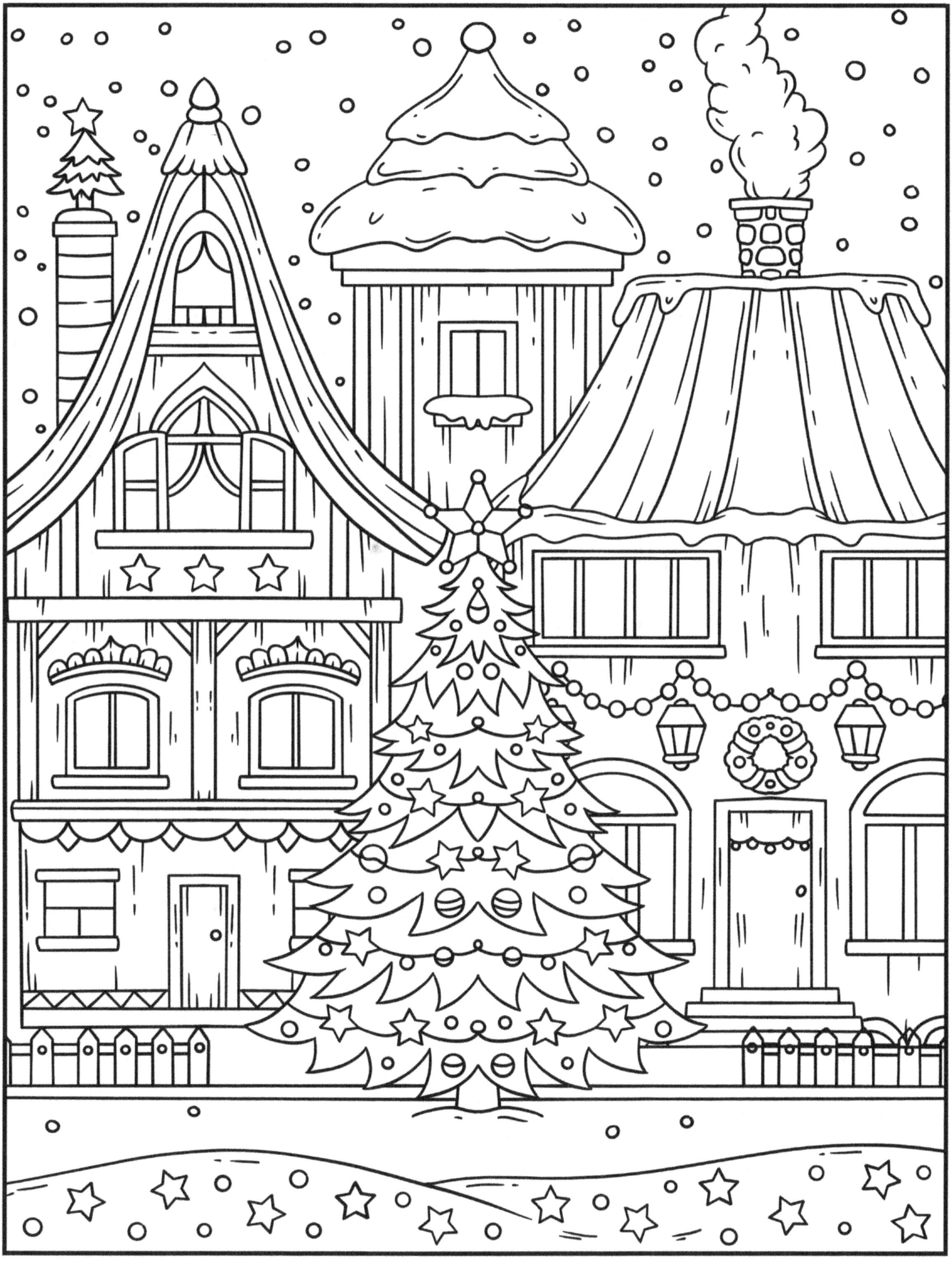

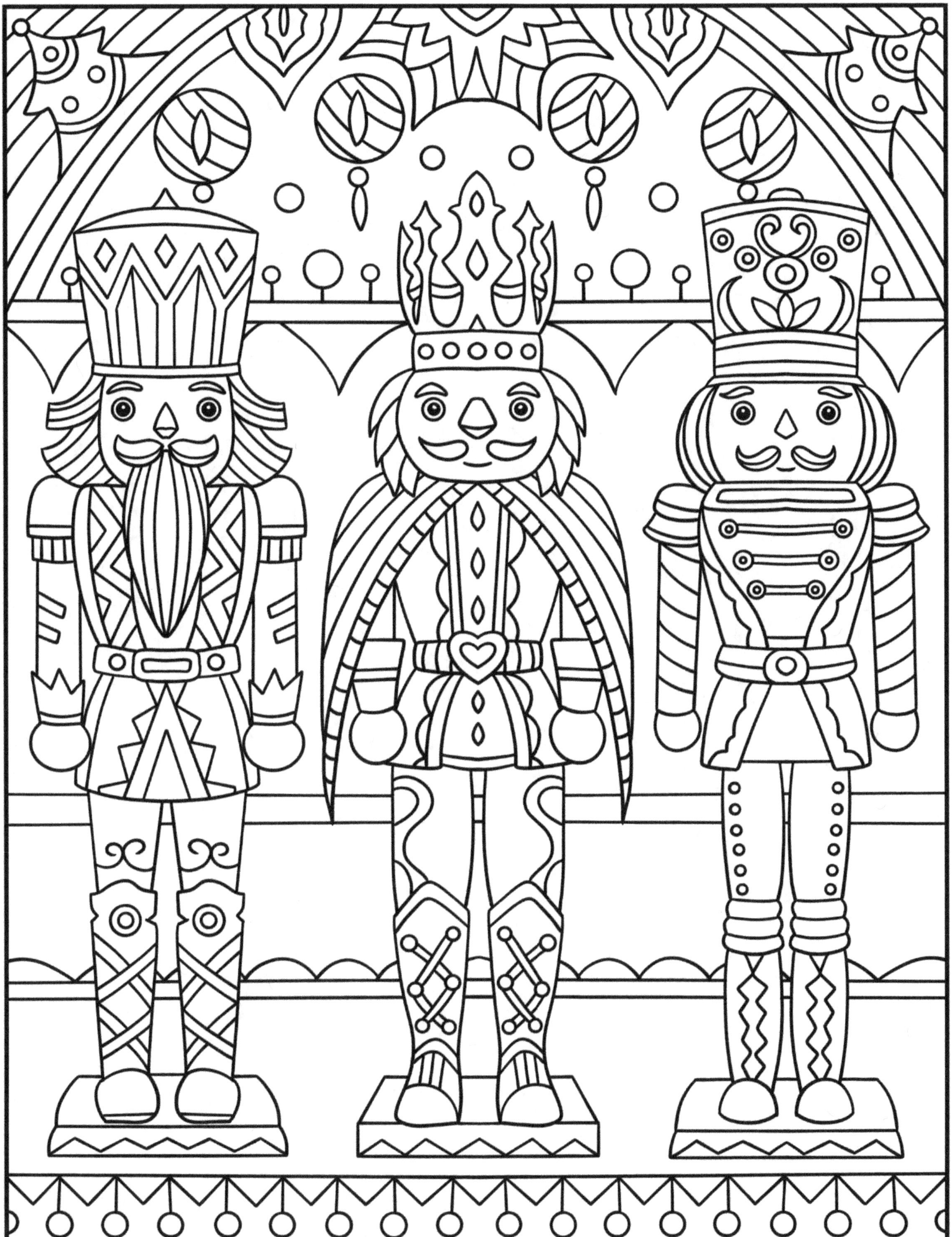

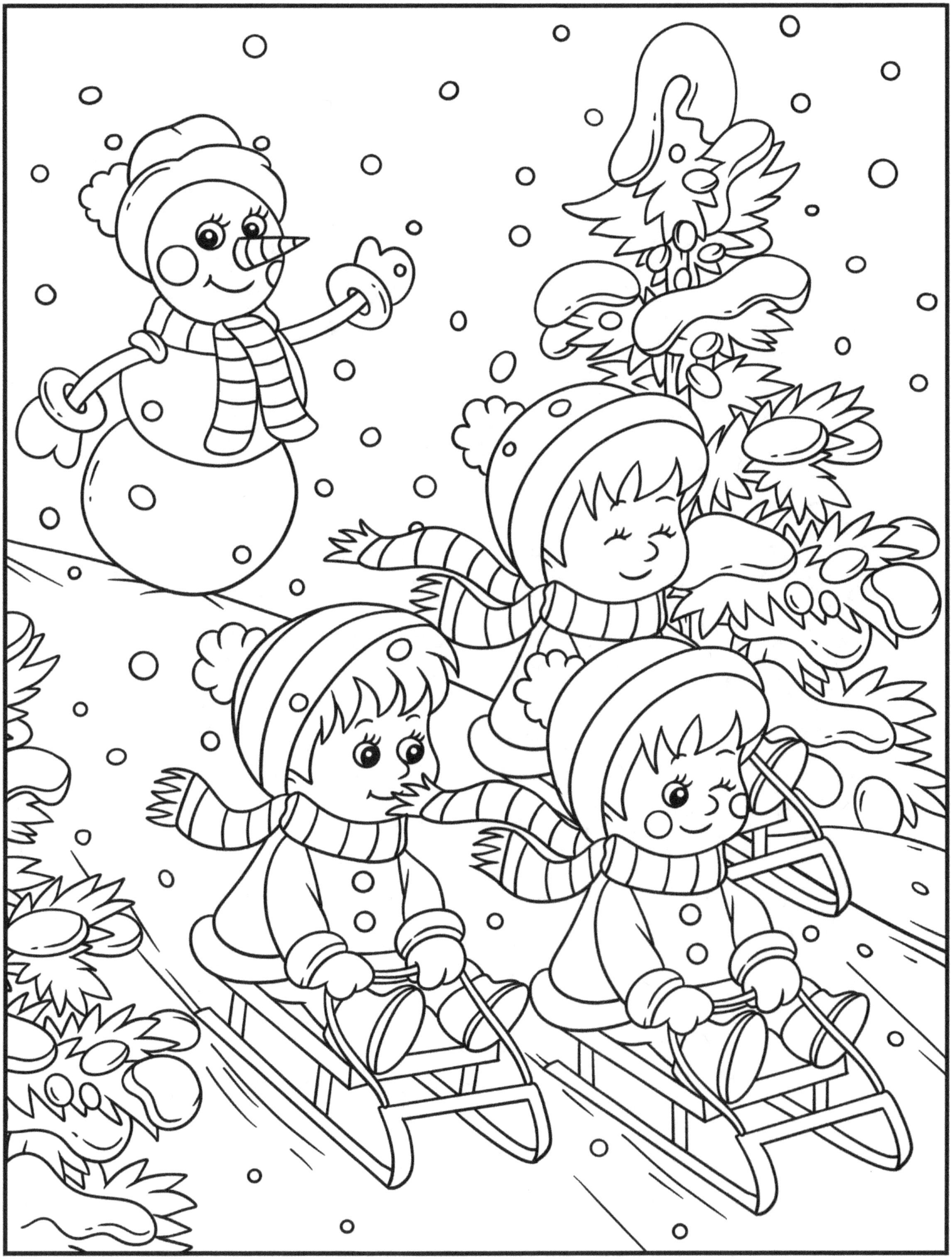

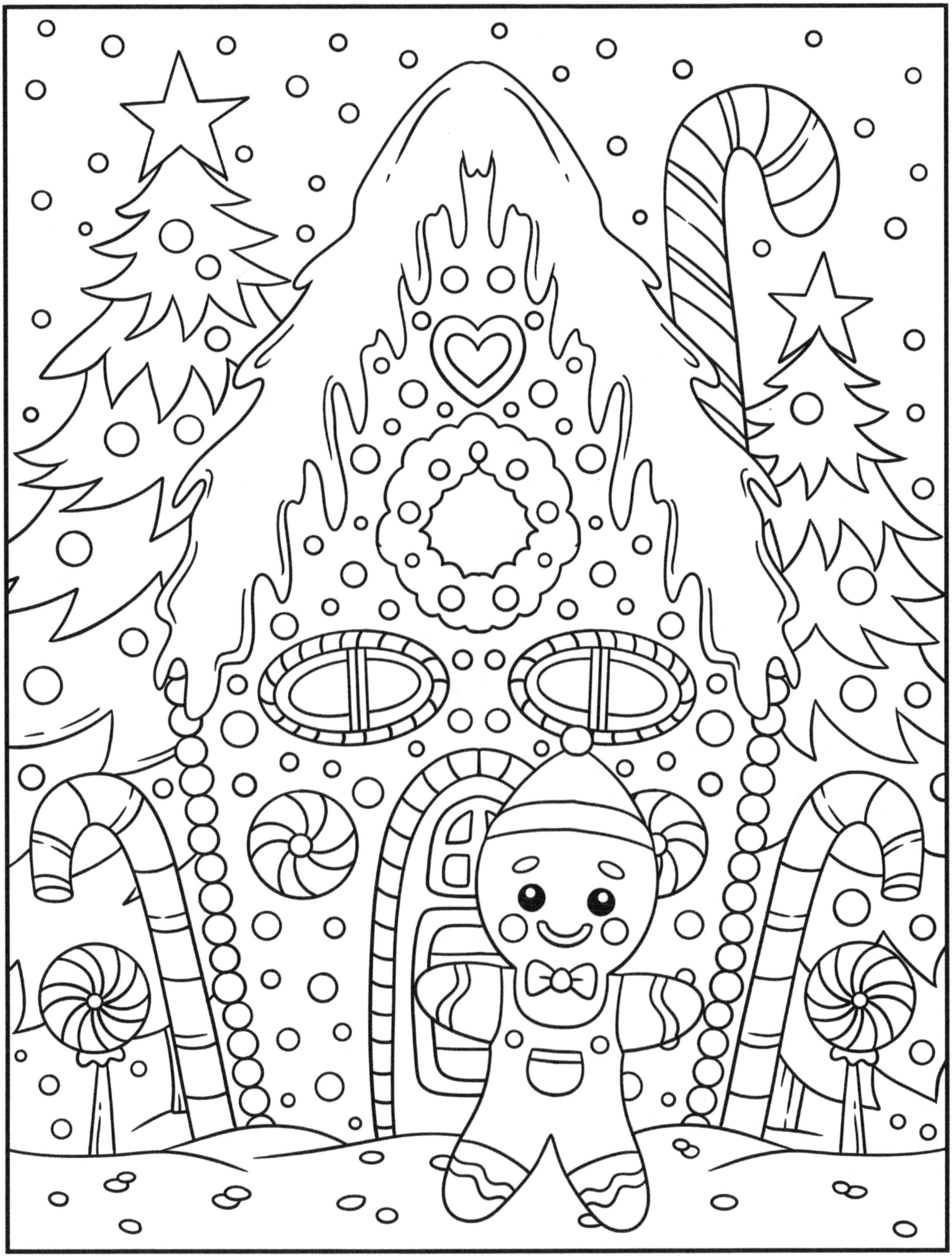

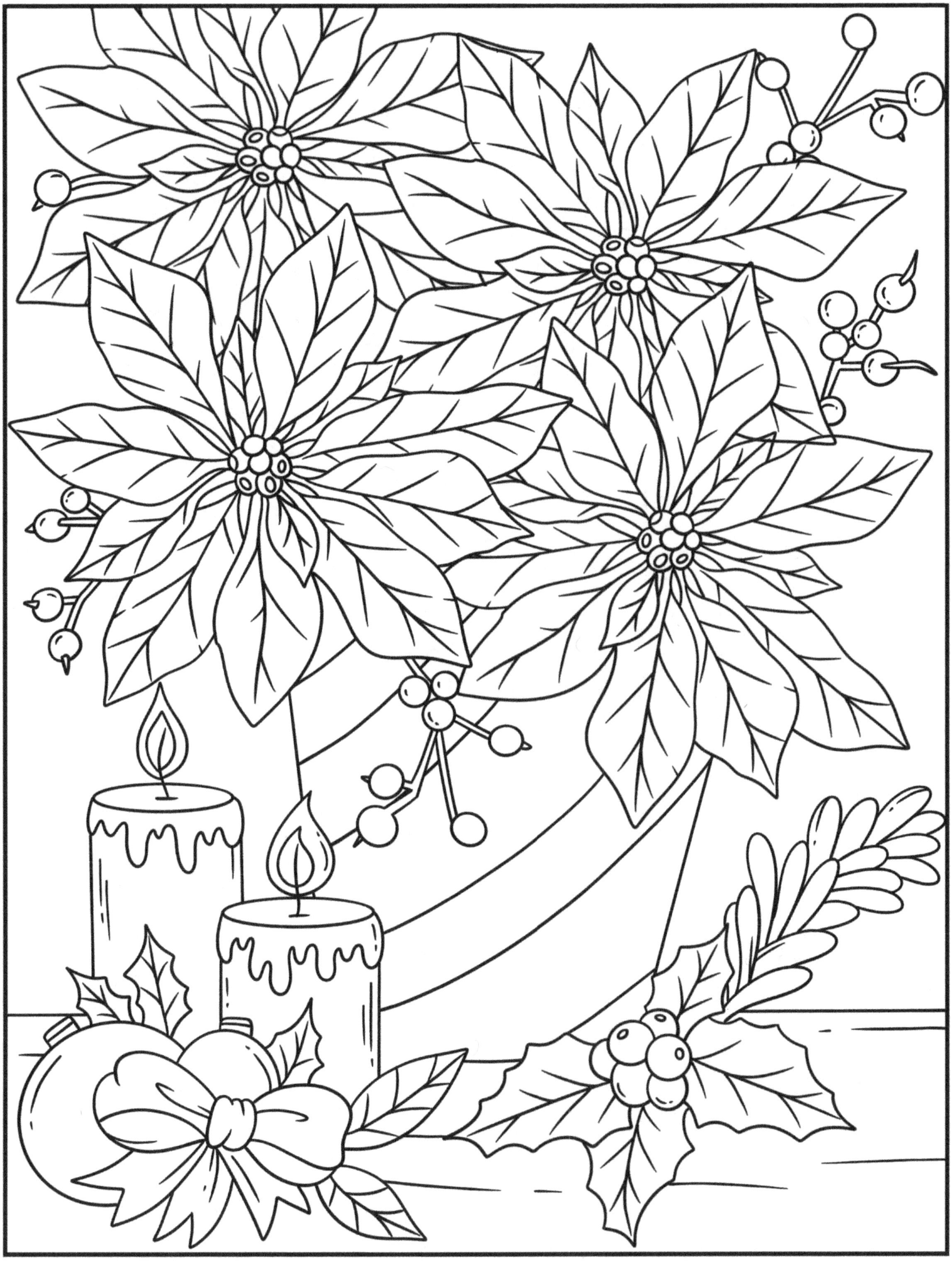

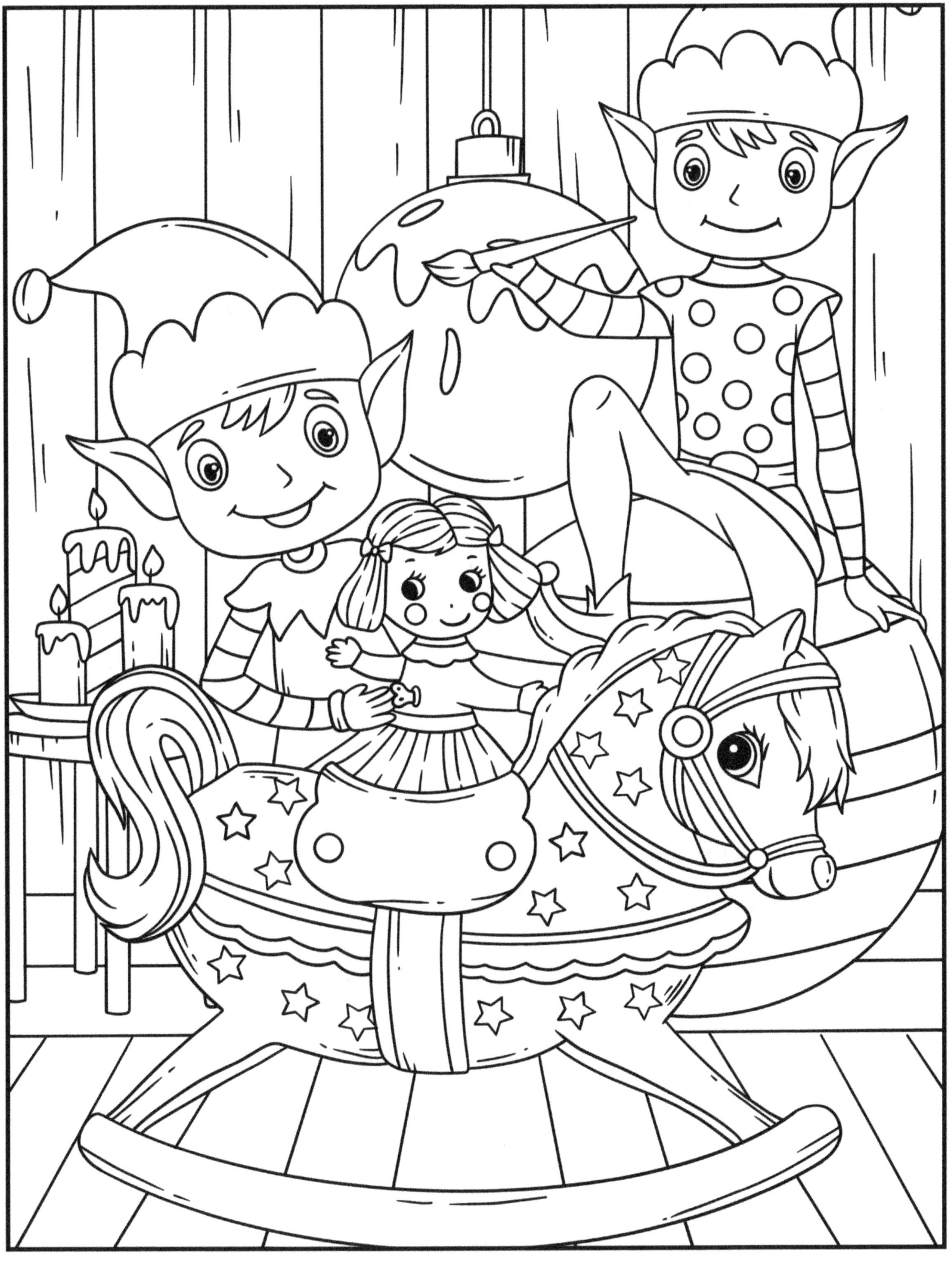

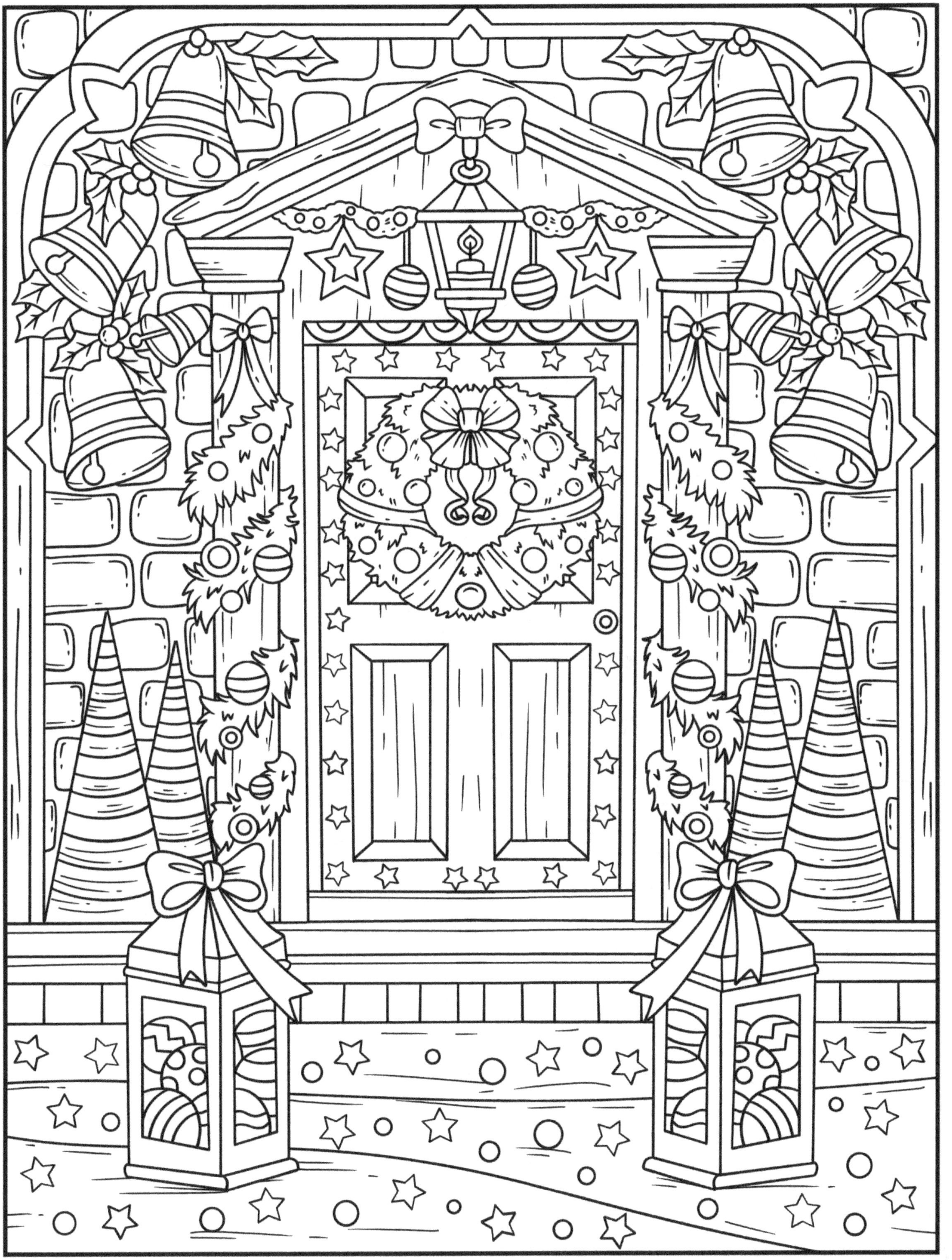

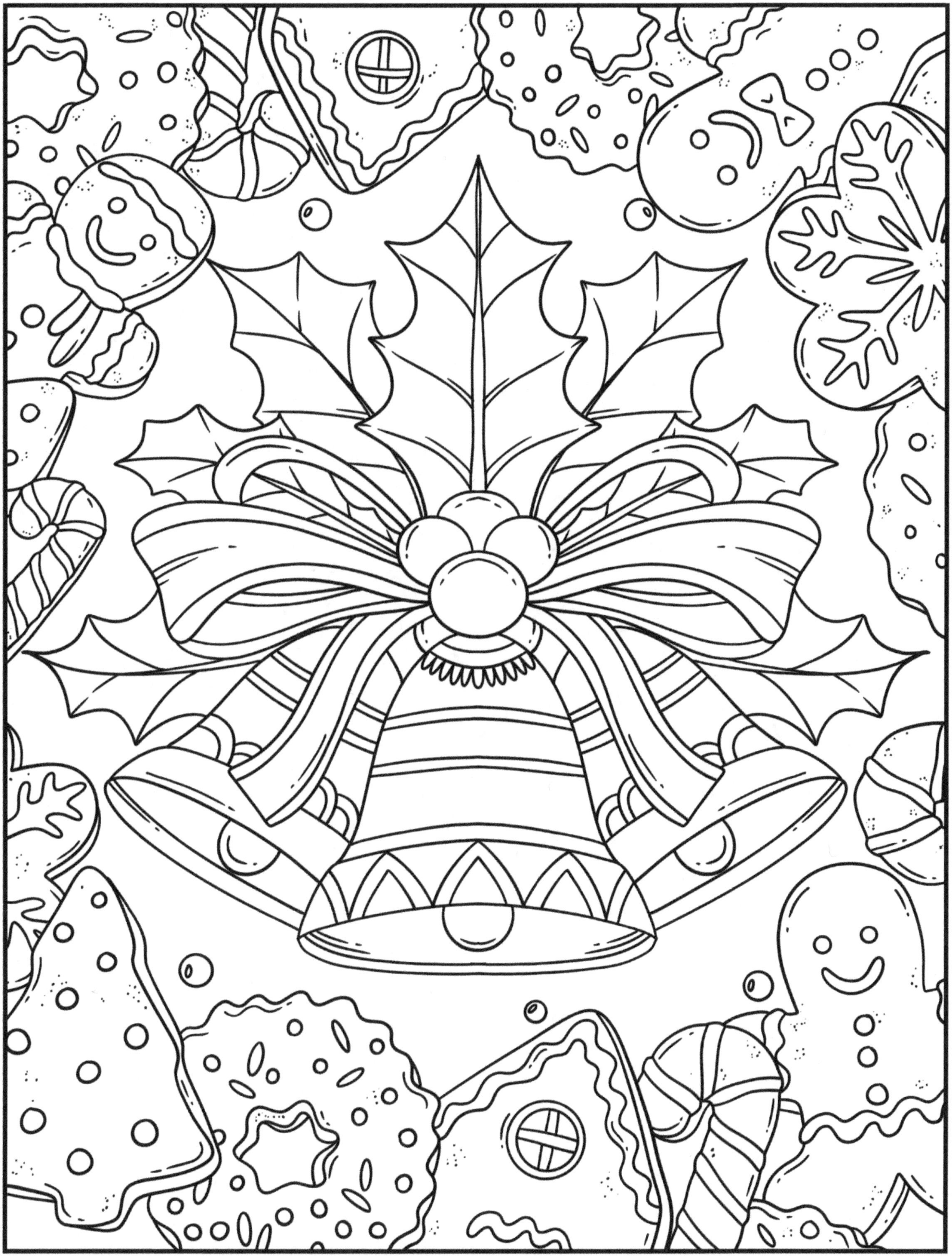

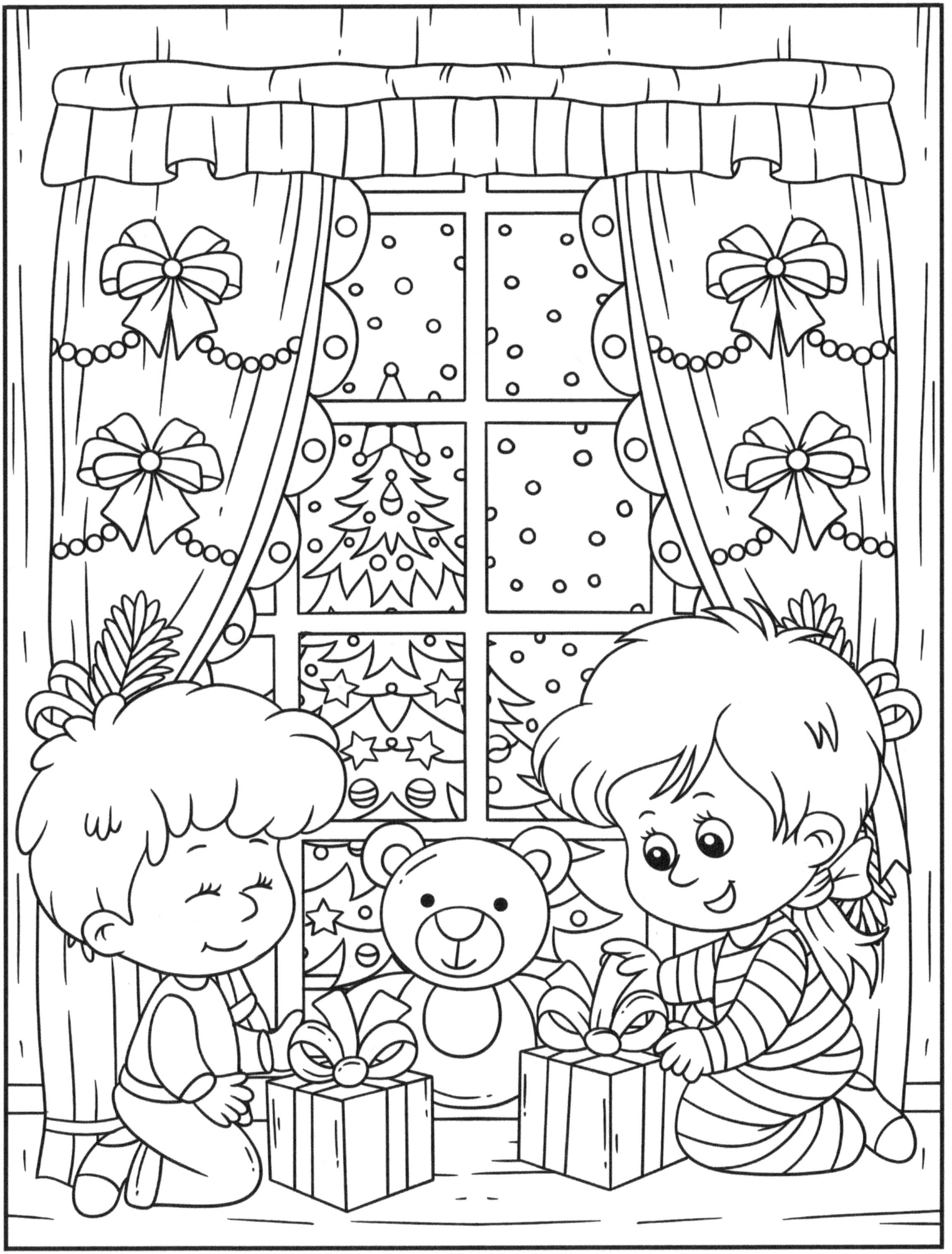

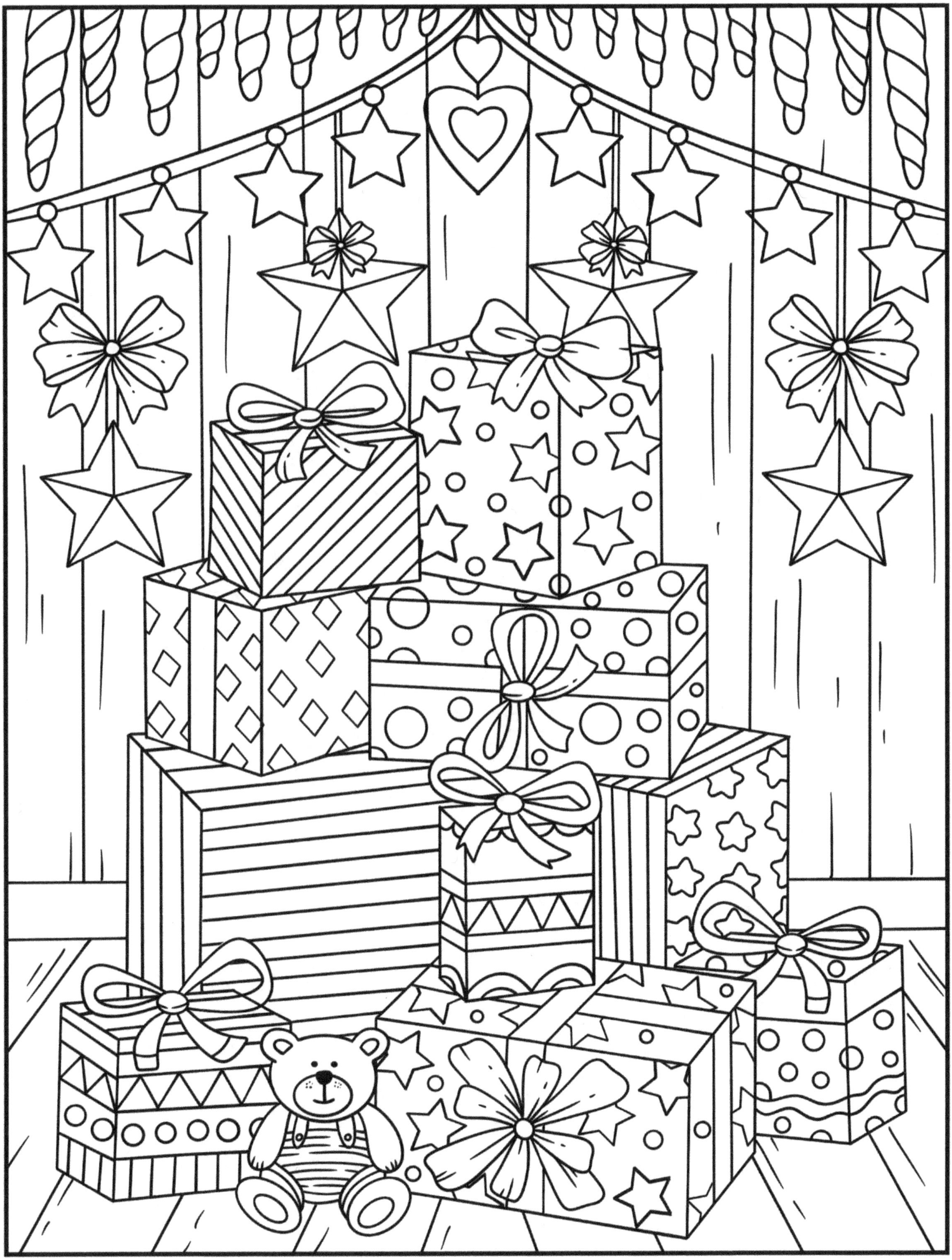

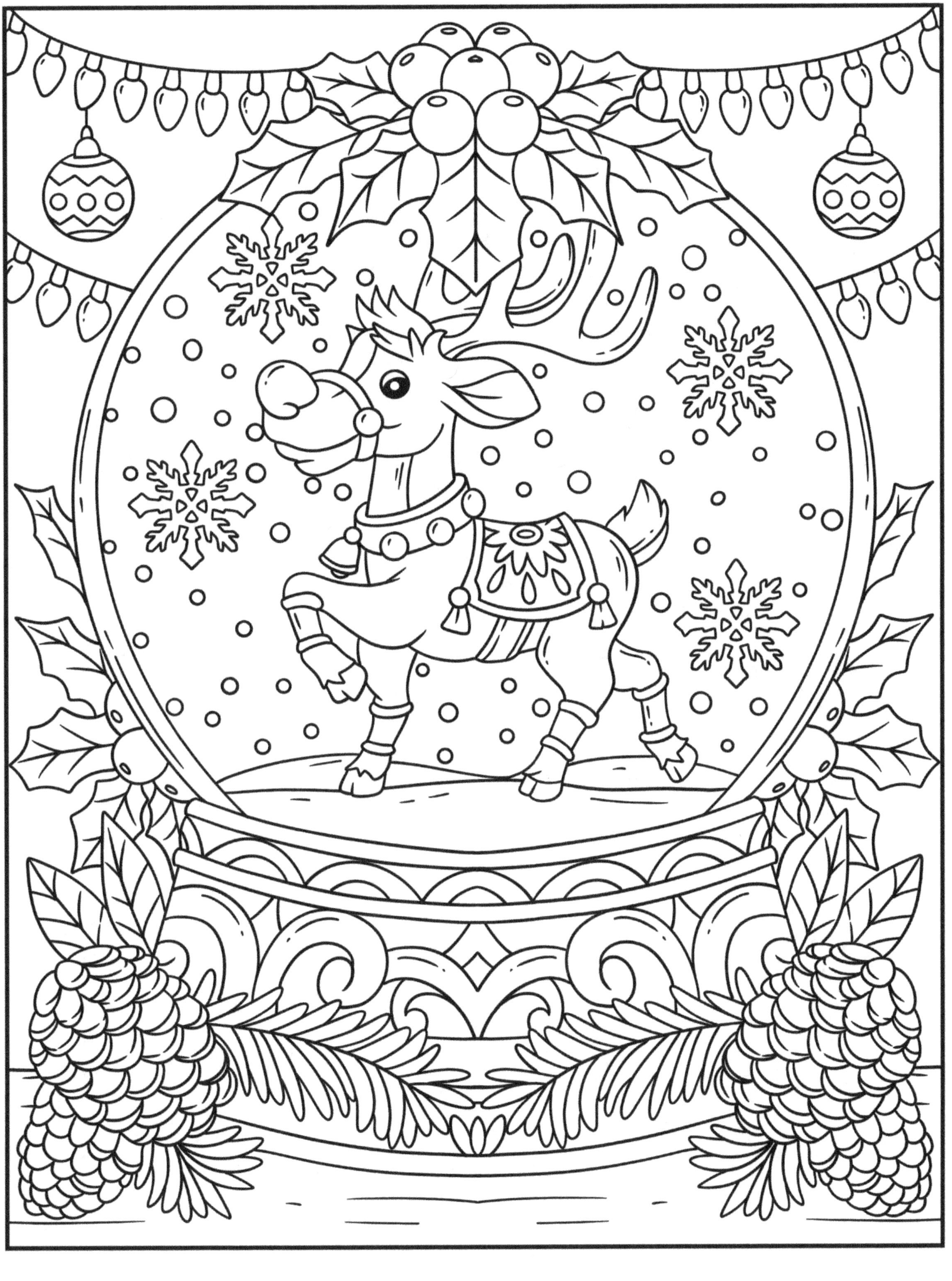

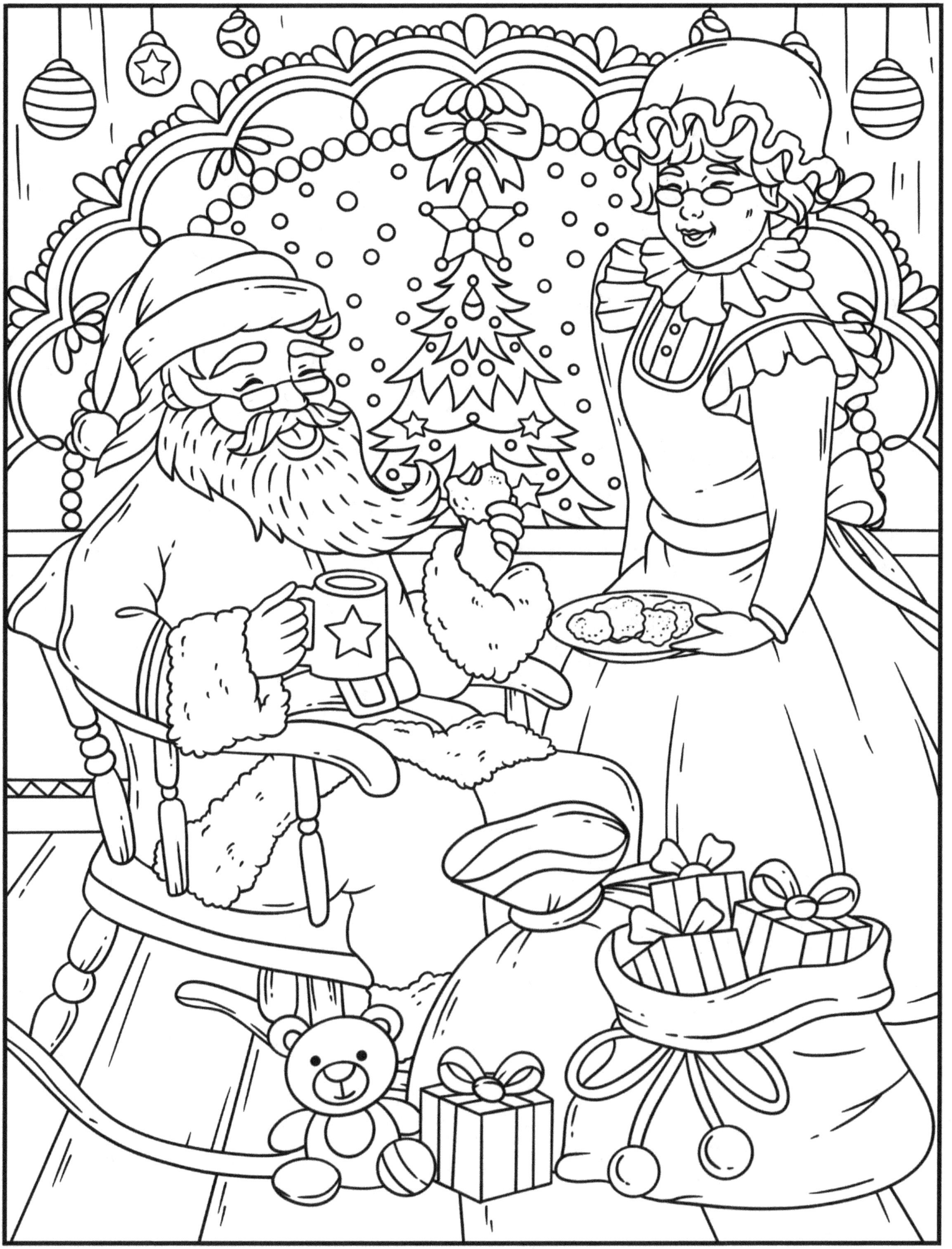

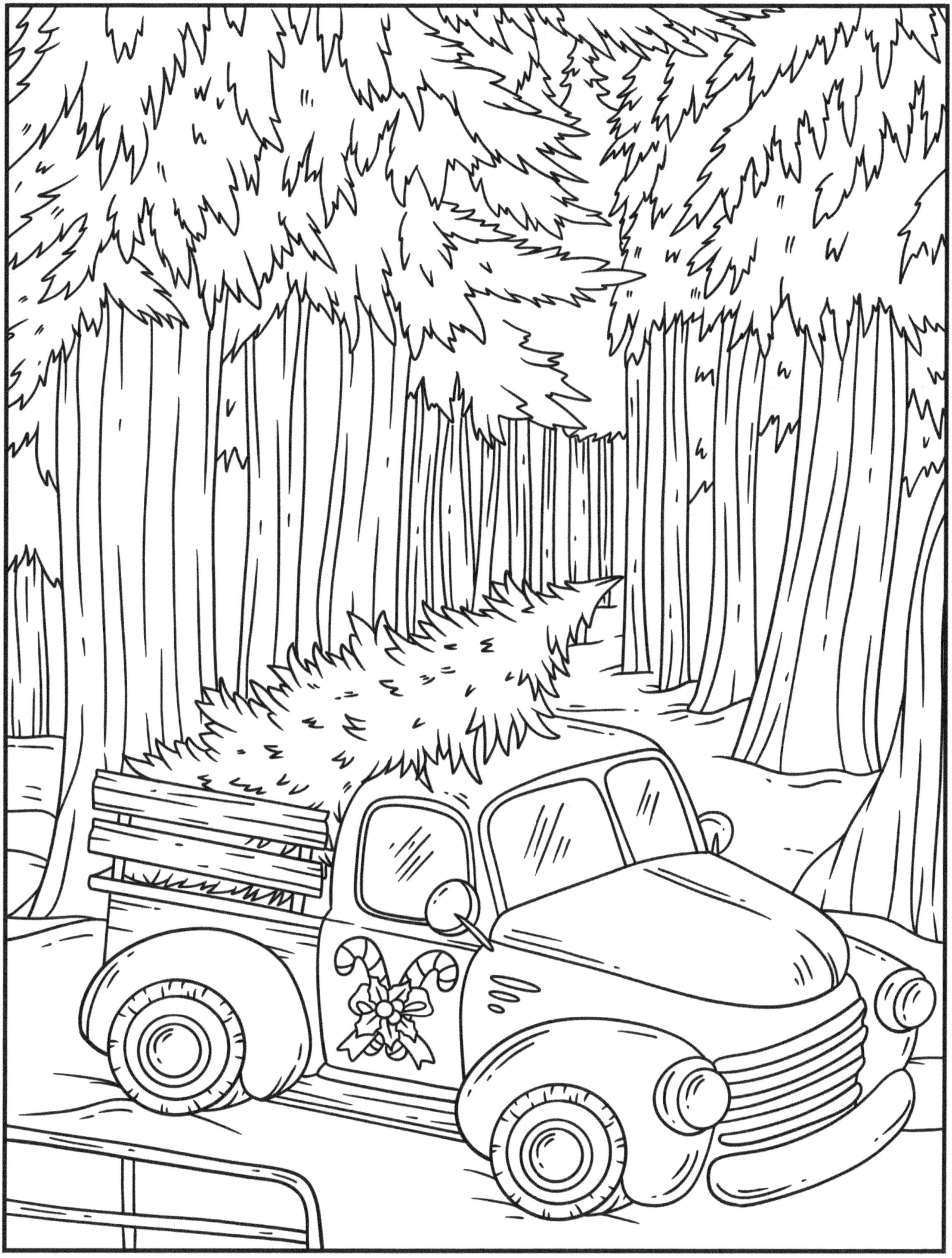

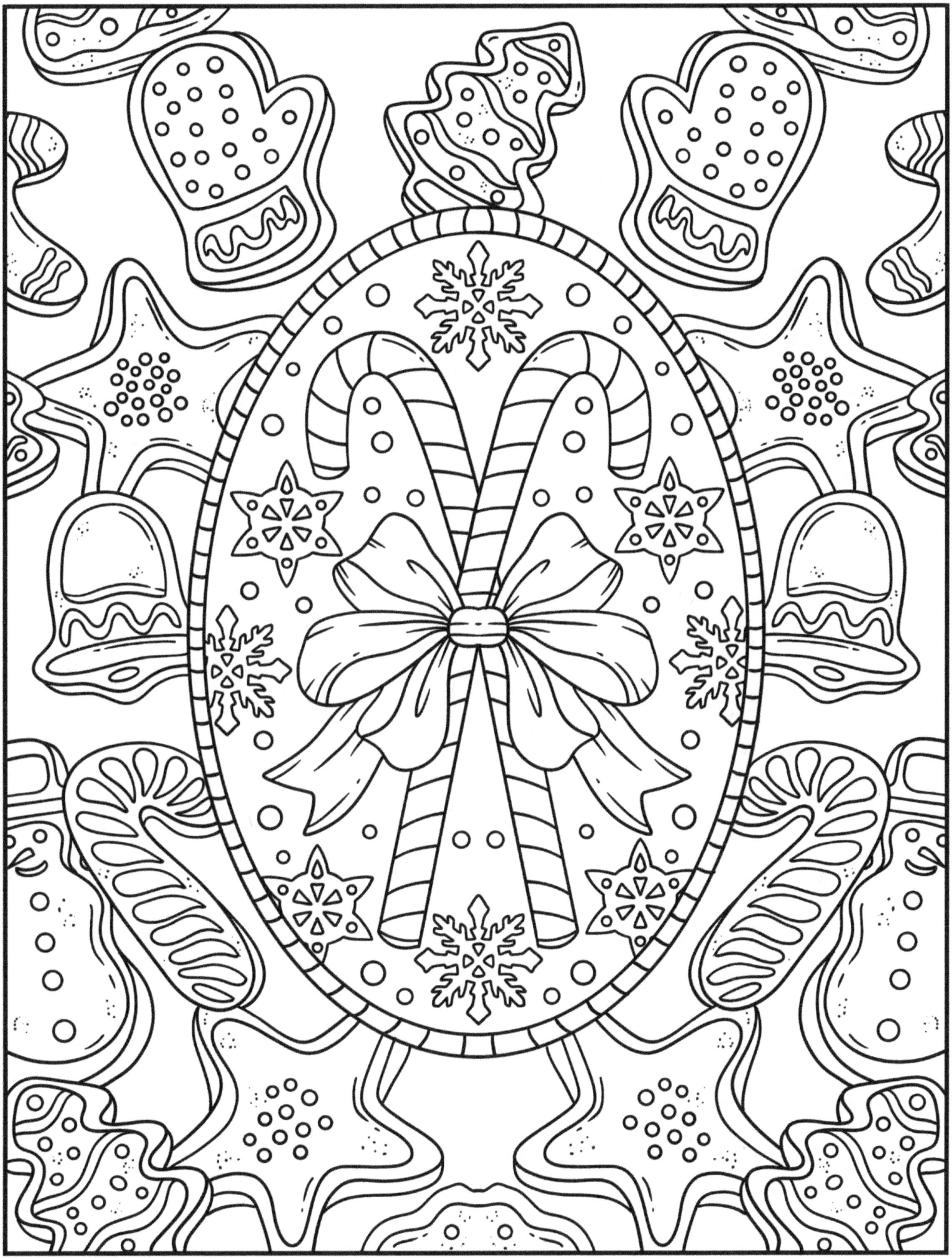

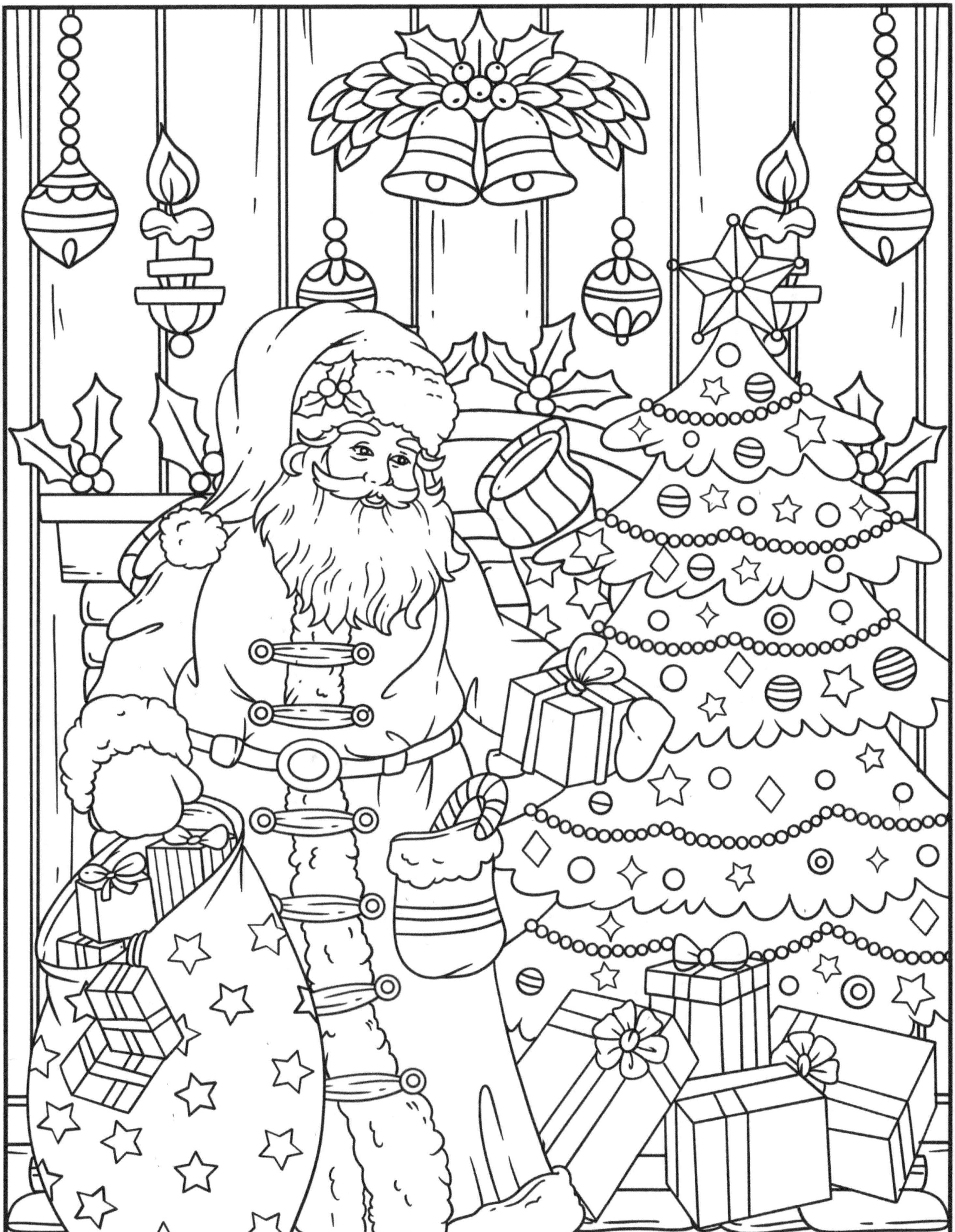

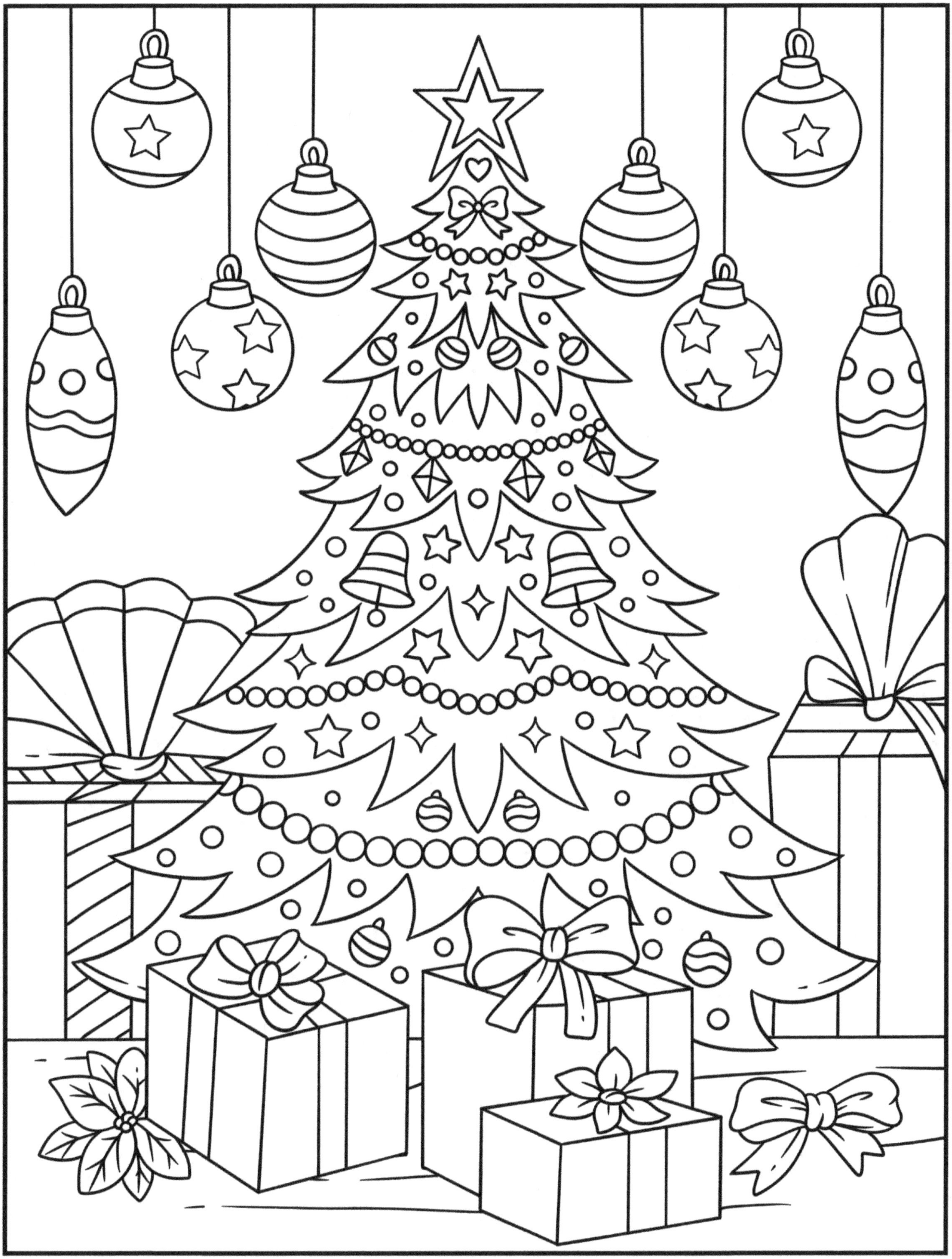

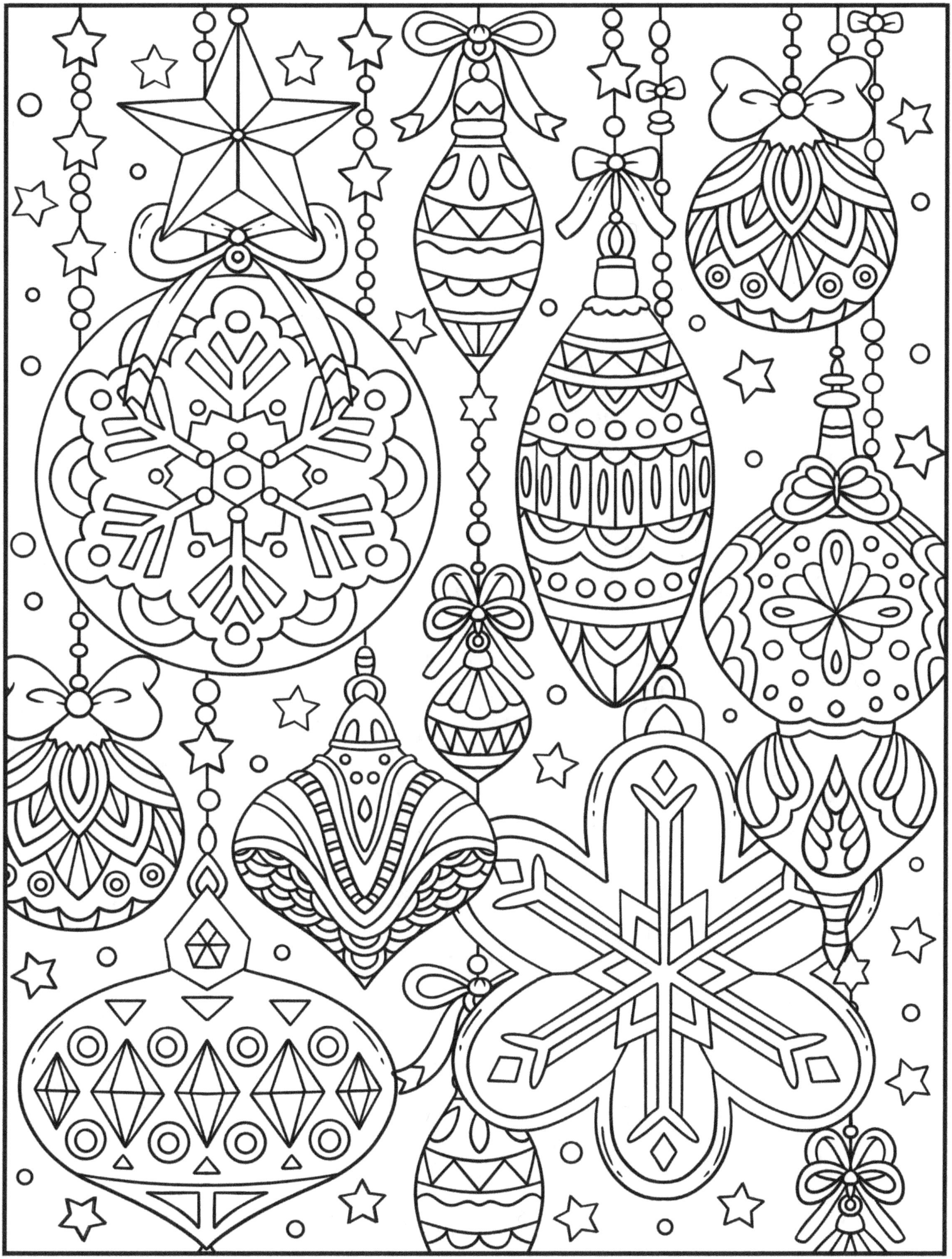

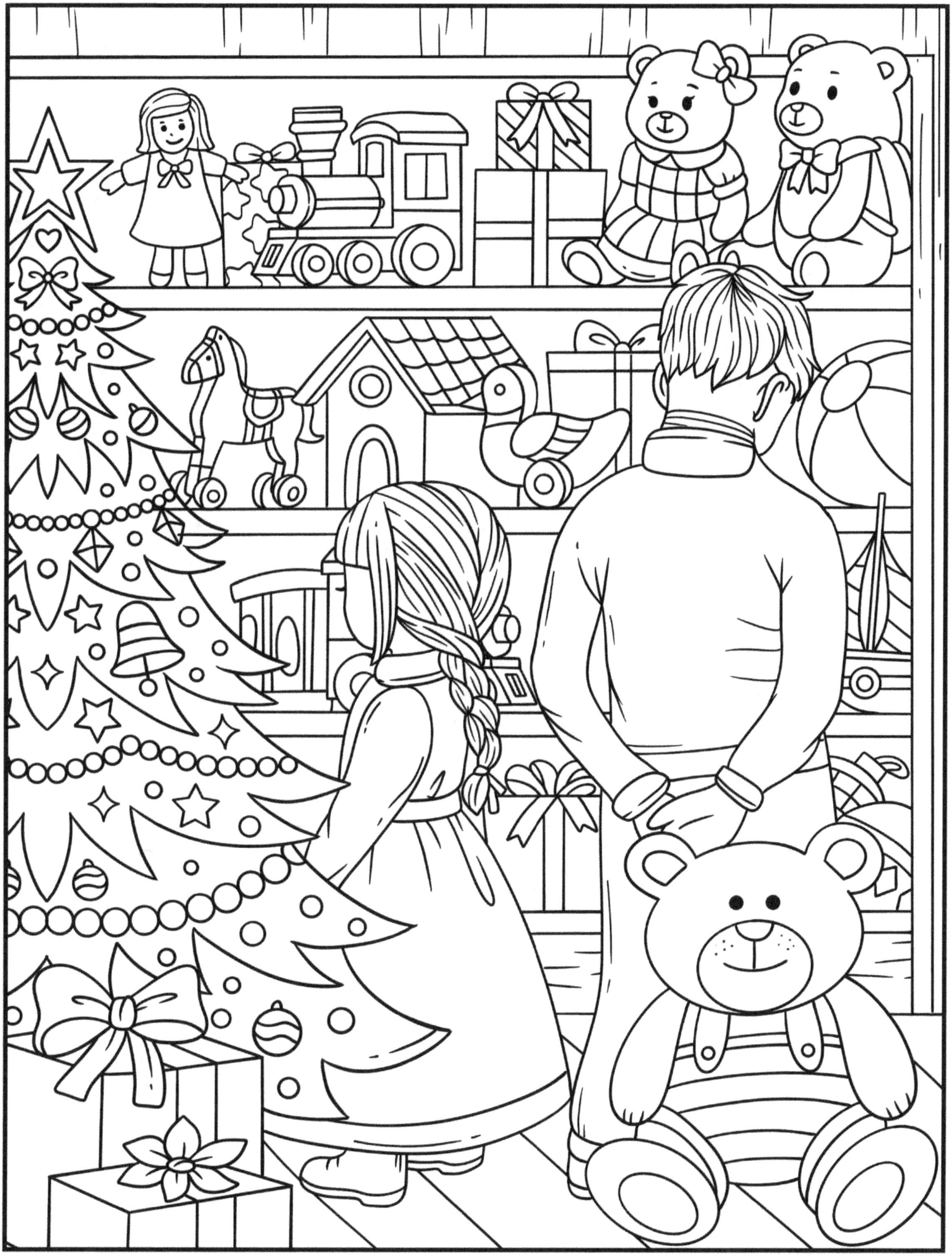

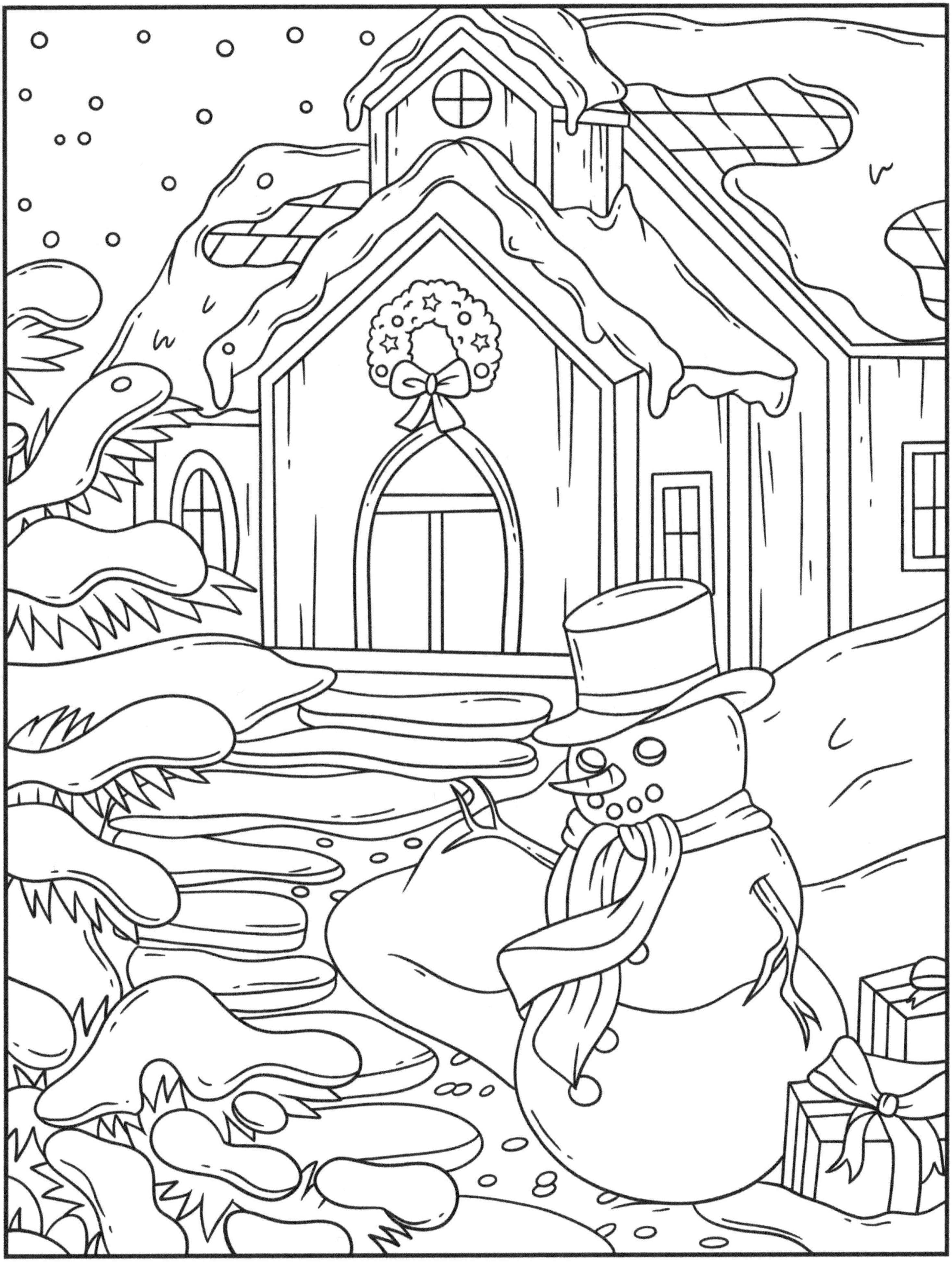

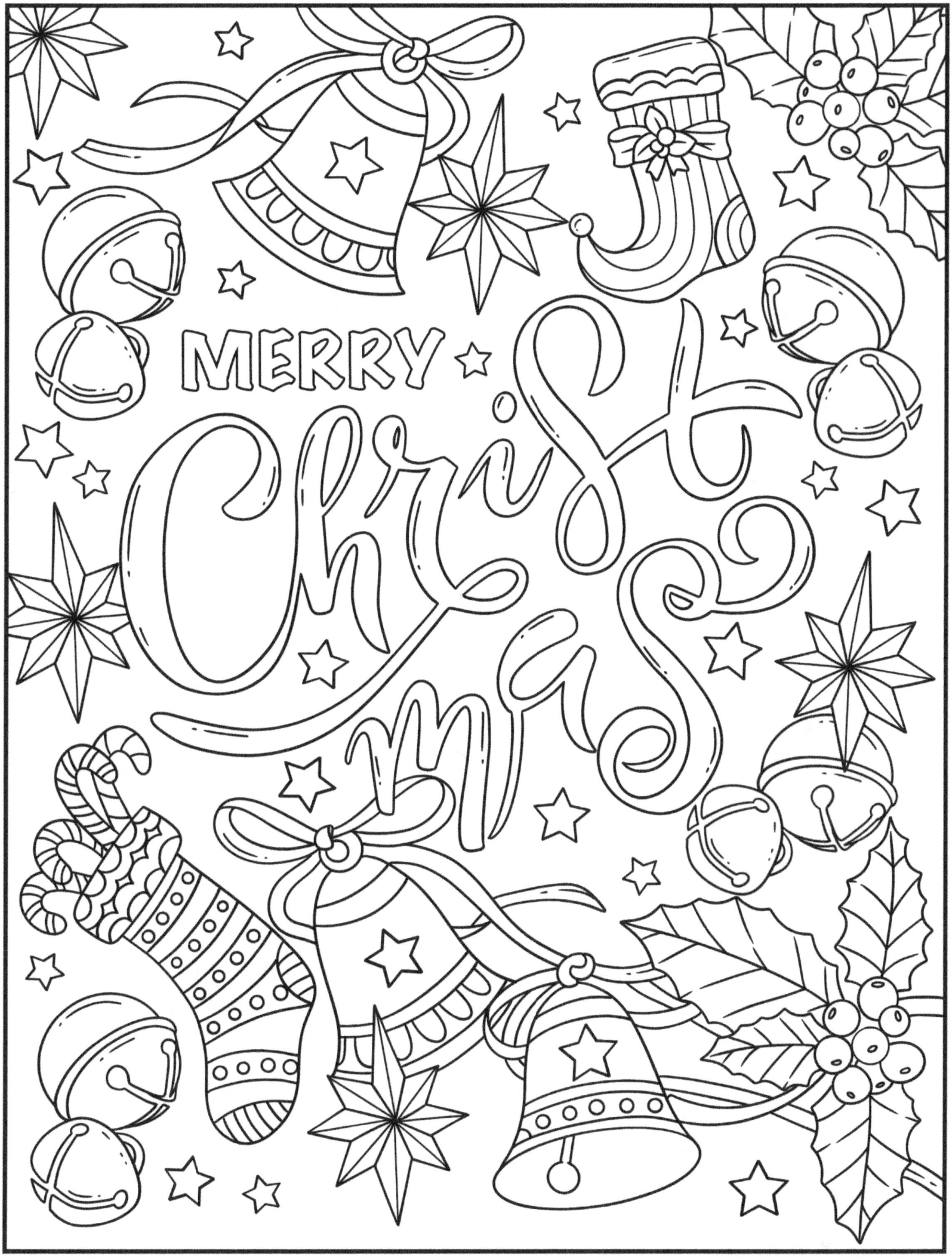
MERRY
Christmas

www.ingramcontent.com/pod-product-compliance
Lightning Source LLC
Chambersburg PA
CBHW080441290526
45791CB00008BA/2568
* 9 7 9 8 8 8 8 9 9 0 0 1 8 *